RESPECTFUL QUERYING
with NUANCE

EBONYE GUSSINE WILKINS

Copyright © 2020 by Ebonye Gussine Wilkins and the Editorial Freelancers Association
Cover and design © 2020 Editorial Freelancers Association
New York, NY

All rights reserved.
No part of this publication may be reproduced, distributed, or transmitted in any form or by any means, including, but not limited to, photocopying, recording, or other electronic or mechanical methods, without the prior written permission of the publisher, except in the case of brief quotations embodied in critical reviews and certain other noncommercial uses permitted by copyright law. For permission requests, write to the publisher at "Attention: Publications Chairperson," at the address below.

266 West 37th St. 20th Floor
New York, NY 10018
office@the-efa.org

ISBN: paperback 978-1-880407-10-3
ISBN: ebook 978-1-880407-14-1

Gussine Wilkins, E. *Respectful Querying with Nuance*

Published in the United States of America by the Editorial Freelancers Association.
Subject Categories: Editing & Proofreading | Communication Studies | Sociolinguistics | Business Skills

Legal Disclaimer
While the publisher and author have made every attempt to verify that the information provided in this book is correct and up to date, the publisher and author assume no responsibility for any error, inaccuracy, or omission.

The advice, examples, and strategies contained herein are not suitable for every situation. Neither the publisher nor author shall be liable for damages arising therefrom. This book is not intended for use as a source of legal or financial advice. Running a business involves complex legal and financial issues. You should always retain competent legal and financial professionals to provide guidance.

EFA Publications Director: Robin Martin
Copyeditor: Leah Rubin
Proofreader: Janet Long
Book Designer: Kevin Callahan | BNGO Books
Cover Designer: Ann Marie Manca

Ebonye Gussine Wilkins
ebonyegussinewilkins.com
inclusivemediasolutions.com

Contents

Introduction	v
The NUANCE Framework	1
N – Notice	3
U – Underscore	7
A – Accept	11
N – Narrow	15
C – Consult	17
E – Empower	21
NUANCE in Practice	25
About the Author	29
About the Editorial Freelancers Association (EFA)	31

Introduction

When most people think of editing, they think about lots of red marks and corrections that make them feel less than smart. Many people feel judged when their writing is edited, particularly because they associate the strength of their writing with the number of red marks that they see. They may not even pay attention to which corrections are made. They will just get overwhelmed by the number of corrections and feel discouraged.

As editors, we are uniquely suited to change this unfortunate perception (arguably, reality) of corrected texts. We shouldn't approach our work as if we are the gatekeepers of grammar and continuity. Writers rely on our insight to produce their best work. The edited result doesn't have to be the most perfect manuscript ever. That should never be the goal of any editorial pursuit. We just need to help the writer put forth the best version of their manuscript. It sounds simple but, as you know, it isn't. Each manuscript is unique like a fingerprint. They may have all the same elements, used recursively, but they are all different.

Each writer has a particular style, and, as editors, you've seen many styles in the manuscripts you've worked on. You've seen writers who love the use of adverbs, or writers who like really big words, or writers whose sentences are embedded clauses that are several layers deep. You've read disjointed thoughts and runaway metaphors and witnessed unsteady replications of structures found in famous works. Armed with your style sheet, you've worked on these manuscripts to impose some order onto them so that they can make sense to you and, of course, the reader.

Here's the thing: The body of publishing professionals working in the United States of America is largely comprised of individuals who are white, straight, cis women, and nondisabled (as defined in the Diversity Baseline Survey 2019 by Lee and Low Books and its co-authors Laura M. Jiménez and Betsy Beckert). It has been that way largely since its inception and hasn't changed very much. Even with a number of visible and invisible movements to publish more diverse books, the landscape hasn't changed much on the editorial side. While technology, including the internet, has lowered the barriers to entry for publishing, it hasn't necessarily leveled the playing field. Many editors that most folks come across are neither people of color nor people from historically marginalized groups. That means that while there are more writers of color producing and publishing work, the chance of their being edited by folks who do not represent their heritages or cultures is quite high.

On the other side of it, much of the literature that is taught in grade school, high school, and college is also written by white individuals. A good portion of the theories and practical applications that are taught reflects a narrow array of literature types and nonfiction texts. These writings often have a white and Western center, perspective, or focus, which means that much of what we are taught about writing and editing has a white (and often straight, cis, and nondisabled) lens. When you get a nonwhite and non-Western writer's work being examined and edited through the lens of a Western perspective, misunderstandings will happen. This often results in over-editing. Over-editing is when too much unnecessary editing is done, which removes the personality and character from the writing.

This is a problem for a few reasons. When writings by nonwhite authors are edited through a white lens, the pieces often get filtered in a way that does not prioritize the writer. One issue can be seen when the editor is regarded as the only relevant expert. Unfortunately, their views and corrections do not always honor and respect the work of the writer. This means that the writer will get back an edited manuscript that doesn't reflect their intentions, vision, or message. This is often demoralizing for a writer. The writer feels misunderstood and sometimes disillusioned because the probable implication is that the writer doesn't know how to write, or that their work is not good enough — or even that

Respectful Querying with NUANCE

their perspective is not valued at all. When editors take a heavy-handed approach to editing and when they dictate more than they query—or query without nuance and respect—the writer has no blueprint on how to move forward. The writer may be left with a manuscript that is a shell of the pre-edited body of work. This is not a win for anyone.

Fortunately, there are things that we can do as editors to avoid this scenario or, at the very least, lessen the well-meaning but negative impact on the work. This is especially important when working with writers from historically marginalized backgrounds.

Querying is a powerful tool that an editor can use to ask questions in a way that allows the writer to see where a reader might get tripped up, or to point out a larger issue, and then offer guidance on what can be done about it. A well-placed query could just be a question posed about continuity or meaning, or it could be the signal of another problem that seems imminent. Whatever the issue is, a query is already a signal that the editor may not exactly know how to resolve it without the author's help. This is okay. It isn't the job of an editor to resolve all the issues in a manuscript. Our job is to give guidance and show the author that they can solve their own writing issues with a bit of guidance.

This involves a mindset shift for the editor so that their instructions and questions remain productive and useful. It involves giving up the idea that the editor is the final authority on a manuscript. The editor should be a partner in the editing and publishing processes—not a gatekeeper. It is a subtle difference, but it can make a huge impact in the long run. Confidence in both the editor to guide and the ability of a writer to resolve manuscript problems will go a long way toward actually leveling the playing field and helping writers publish with their knowledge and intentions left largely intact. To facilitate helping writers retain the intangibles that make their work reflective of themselves, editors should approach editing with NUANCE.

The NUANCE Framework

NUANCE is a framework that allows editors to check their biases when offering editorial assistance by using thoughtful queries that allow writers to understand what kind of help is being offered and why. This will allow writers to understand the thoughts behind the queries so they can make decisions on accepting editorial assistance that may clarify and preserve the author's intentions and work.

Each letter in NUANCE is a reminder of what the editor should keep in mind:

N – Notice
U – Underscore
A – Accept
N – Narrow
C – Consult
E – Empower

Each chapter in this booklet will explore one letter and offer a starting point for querying with respect and grace. Editors should be able to use the framework to construct thoughtful queries that allow the editor to assist rather than obstruct. Over time, editing and querying with NUANCE will sharpen an editor's thought processes and become a useful tool for working on fiction and nonfiction manuscripts.

But we don't want to just write regular or basic queries. We want to write powerful queries that give us a window to better understand the manuscript through the eyes of the author. We also want to sketch a plan to work with the information we've gathered. We want to build a blueprint that allows us to continue to offer the guidance that is necessary to polish a manuscript, but also helps the author make the final decisions. While better is relative and will look different in each manuscript, there is still a lot we can do to move forward.

In building respectful queries with NUANCE, we will use each letter to remind us of what we can do, why we should be doing it, and how to do it well.

For each letter, we should take an action and consider the approach for that action. The "action" is the prompt (gentle reminder) of what you should be considering, and the approach helps us do it tactfully.

N – Notice

As an editor, noticing things is basically your job description. You have to notice if a comma is in the right place, if the third person past or the subjunctive is being used, or even if the dots are being connected for the reader. By noticing things and fixing them when needed—or querying them as appropriate—you are able to help the writer meet their goals.

The part that people rarely talk about is that noticing things draws directly on your knowledge of the subject matter. When it comes to comma usage or incorrect tenses, or even if a text is mixing up rules from different style guides, you will notice when something is wrong—if you know what you are looking for. For the mechanics and grammar of Standard American English, you've got it covered. If you are a newer editor, you already have the rules and tools that you need to enforce order on a manuscript. If you are a more experienced editor, you may see some rules being broken and decide that it is okay because it makes sense for the context. Overall, the writer is paying you for your judgment on how to make a manuscript the best version of itself (whether or not they realize or acknowledge this). With some exceptions, the writer is trusting that your judgment is sound and that you won't do any harm to their manuscript. Most writers and editors think that by not introducing errors into a manuscript, and eliminating the ones that are there, you are not doing any harm to the manuscript.

This is not necessarily the case.

Mechanics aside, there is a lot that can be done that will unravel the spine of a manuscript. I don't mean the physical spine that holds a book together, but the intangible structure that may or may not be readily apparent. Truth is, if it's a structure that you've encountered before—likely from your training as an editor, a writer, or as an avid reader—you will notice it right away and either fix it or leave a remark about what you think is going on.

But what happens when you notice something is off, but you aren't sure which part is the problem? Your "inner ear" (this is what I call the grammar in your head—the one you learned to speak with, not the one you learned to write with) is telling you that something is not what you expected. This is your editorial instinct. Your editorial instinct, if gently cultivated and nurtured, may be quite reliable. However, you may find that the tools that you normally use to resolve an issue in a manuscript don't quite fit. You may even slowly realize that you don't know what is going on. You just know that something isn't right.

Now, let's examine what "something isn't right" means. To know if something is wrong, you have to know what is right—what something is supposed to be. This is sometimes referred to as the canonical position. For example, if you see a chair that is upright with all four legs on the ground in a way that makes the chair ready to accept a sitter, you will know that it is "right." The way the chair is positioned allows it to bear the weight of the sitter. Unless it is broken or damaged, and as long as it is on a firm, flat surface, you wouldn't expect any problems with it. You can reliably sit on the chair and expect all to be well. However, if only two of the legs are on the firm, flat surface, or if a leg is missing, or if the chair has its legs parallel to the floor instead of perpendicular, you will know something is not right. You might even know how to fix it (set it upright on a firm, flat surface so that all four legs are perpendicular to the floor). If the chair didn't have a back, or if it were a three-legged stool instead of a standard chair, you'd still likely be able to identify this variation and adjust accordingly.

All of the information that you know about a chair is based on exposure to what a chair is, its canonical position, what it looks like when it is not in its canonical position, and some information on what to do when it is not. It is information that was fed to you, likely in your infancy, and reinforced over time. Writing and grammar isn't all that different from that. In fact, you started learning the rules of grammar and language in your infancy! Everything you know is based on prior information of what something is and what it should look like. You have a pool of information to draw from to put the pieces together.

This is how editing usually works. You know what the parts look like, their variations, the rules that govern them, and what to do if there is an unexpected occurrence (something deviates from what you would expect). You notice something because you have the background information to do so. This is why you are able to fix sentences and manuscripts of all lengths and structures.

Truth is, storytelling, language usage, and structures can vary from language to language and culture to culture. Yes, there are commonalities, and you may be able to predict a lot of them (after all, that's what linguistics is all about). This predictability of what to expect with language is largely a result of what you were taught as an editor, a writer, or a reader. What you encounter is likely expected based on your training and your exposure to how sentences, paragraphs, and larger works are structured.

What happens if a writer—for example, a writer of color—sends you something that doesn't match anything else you've ever encountered before? It will certainly be something that you notice. You notice it simply because it deviates from your expectation.

So, what do you do now? That's easy. You write a query and ask questions! You can either ask the author for more information or point out what you've noticed and make the author aware of it.

And yes, this is where (and when) you can start building your query. The table in this chapter offers a starting point for building queries with NUANCE. (There is a table for each letter in NUANCE and the table for each letter can be found in the corresponding chapters.) Use the suggestions in the tables to build thoughtful, actionable queries to help your author do their best work under your guidance.

Your Action: Notice what is unfamiliar.
Your Approach: Think *Technical*.

The "technical" approach is to think about the big picture of the possible issue that you want to draw attention to. For this part of the query, we are getting very general about what we are noticing. "Think Technical" just means to categorize the kind of issue it is. Is it an issue of grammar that may be regional but necessary to the context? Then it is a grammar issue. Is there content in one part that doesn't match or make sense for related content that's in close proximity to the passage in question? Then it is likely a continuity issue. When starting your query, think about what kind of technical issue it could be, and use that to point out what you've noticed.

	What to Do	**How to Phrase It**
N – Notice	**Think *Technical*:** Highlight the relevant parts of the text. **Ask Yourself:** Is it grammar, language, context, unfamiliar content, or is something missing or incorrect?	I noticed that . . . I'm observing that . . . It's notable that . . .

U – Underscore

Noticing content that needs to be addressed is the first step. If you've used the table in the Notice chapter, then you've already identified the content you want the author to pay special attention to by highlighting it. Now, you have to get specific on why you chose to point out the potential issue in the first place.

You may not yet understand why you noticed something. It might require a little work to get closer to the reason. As you re-read the portion you highlighted from the "Notice" exercise, you will want to underscore the parts that are giving you pause. If you are still not sure what to underscore, consider the following questions.

Does the highlighted passage or content have major grammar issues?

Does the passage use language that you are not familiar with?

Do you think that the passage uses language that may not be appropriate for the context?

Is there a shift in setting that you do not understand?

Is there any surrounding content that hints at something not lining up with the passage that you highlighted?

Is the highlighted content a minor detail that upsets the surrounding text, or does it seem like something bigger is happening that affects the "spine" of the work?

Do you think there is readily accessible information that could give context to the problem that isn't already directly linked?

Do you think that the highlighted text is beyond your scope of knowledge and that you will not be able to resolve it at all?

These questions are important as they are qualitative. These are questions that any editor should ask themselves when editing something that is outside of their cultural experiences or just requires knowledge that the editor may not have. You have to be able to identify why something doesn't make sense to you. In the Notice section, you highlighted the what. In the Underscore section, you highlight the why.

It is important to recognize that anything that you highlight might seem like a really big thing at first. That's okay. The initial highlight is for you to just get a quick visual assessment of how big the "issue" is. Then you should run through the aforementioned questions to get an idea of what exactly is bothering you. It is also important to understand that what you think is an issue may not be an issue at all! When you write any query, there is always at least a doubt or unknown that needs to be addressed. The unknown element here should not stress you out or excessively frustrate you. You may not know the answer, and you want to find out, so you will leave a query. However, getting clear on what you think needs addressing is the first step toward being able to offer guidance to the author.

As you think about what you want to address, you may need to make some notes on the side about which of the questions may apply. Is it one issue, or a number of issues? If it is only one or two, then just mark them down and then step away from the section or manuscript—and come back at a later point. If it is more than a couple of possible issues, then mark those down as well and come back to see if you can eliminate some of the possibilities. After some time away, you may find that it has fewer points to address than you originally thought.

With unfamiliar texts, it is important to review and revisit the text. Give yourself time to think about it. That space can often do wonders for pinpointing issues.

Your Action: Underscore the parts that you think need to be addressed.
Your Approach: Think Qualitative.

Respectful Querying with NUANCE

	What to Do	**How to Phrase It**
U – Underscore	**Think *Qualitative*:** Underscore the "biggest" issues that you can identify.	In particular, it seems like [passage] is [qualitative descriptor] because . . .
	Ask Yourself: Is it a cultural reference that you do not understand? Is it inconsistent? Is it disconnected from something mentioned earlier?	Specifically, the [passage] could be seen as [qualitative] and . . .

A – Accept

After you've had the time to review and think about what you've underscored, it is time to accept that you may not be able to solve the problem on your own.

For this kind of work, a mindset shift is required. It doesn't have to be a huge change. It's just one change — but with that change comes acceptance. As an editor, the author hired you because they wanted to benefit from your editorial expertise. You took the project on because you are confident that you can help the writer fix and adjust their manuscript so that it is readable and understandable. But when it comes to certain content — especially content reflective of cultural knowledge, language usage, certain grammar rules, or specific backgrounds and expertise — you may not know what is truly going on in the context.

This is the part that you need to accept.

You can be the best editor in your field, or a newer editor in your chosen industry. You may even be a mid-career editor for general editing jobs. But you will not know everything. You will not be able to solve every single editorial problem or fix every perceived or actual editorial issue.

This is okay. It is okay to not be able to solve every editorial puzzle.

Sometimes the joy of editing comes from the satisfaction of resolving a problem within a text. Smoothing out a manuscript can be very gratifying. But if you've come across a piece that just doesn't match your expertise (and you are already knee-deep in the manuscript) then you will have to give up the idea that you can fix everything. You do not have to be an expert in everything.

It is also important to know and understand that you are not the best editor for every manuscript. In many cases, there are editors out there (who you may not know or know of) that are better suited to handle the manuscript that you are working on. For any number of reasons, the project came to you.

Whenever possible, you should pass along a lead to another editor who is better suited for the job. It's the editorial version of "do no harm" in a sense. An editor that is better suited to handle certain kinds of manuscripts will be able to work with the particularities of a job that require their expertise. However, as some legacies of editorial networks may keep editors from similar backgrounds in the same circles, you may not know of editors that would be better suited for a project. This is a common problem which requires a long-term solution: expand your network of editors. In the meantime, you can accept that you can still help a writer do their best work if you approach the project with care. Good judgment, a bit of humility, and a willingness to query in a helpful but judicious manner will go a long way toward meeting a writer's needs in a scenario like this one. You can still make a positive difference in a manuscript with the expertise that you do have. You still have knowledge that will be useful to the author.

Remember, you are the guide that the writer hired to shepherd them through this process. Guidance is what you really provide anyway. Guidance through targeted and thoughtful querying is a practical solution to making the manuscript better. Sure, a lot of times you are absolutely correct about the suggestions that you make to improve writing. However, those are just suggestions, and the writer can reject them as they see fit. So, when you accept that you can't solve every issue, know that you can still guide a writer and be helpful in their journey toward publication. There is still work that you can do!

But you can't be an effective guide until you help narrow down what can be done to set the manuscript and author up for success.

Your Action: Accept that you may not understand everything in the text.

Your Approach: Think Practical.

Respectful Querying with NUANCE

	What to Do	**How to Phrase It**
A – Accept	**Think *Practical*:** Acknowledge that you may not have enough information to handle a problem's resolution. **Ask Yourself:** Am I offering a fix to resolve the possible issue or am I offering guidance for next steps?	This requires your input to resolve/reconcile . . . How we move forward on this depends on your answers to the following questions . . . (Use if you have follow-up questions.)

N – Narrow

So far, you've noticed a technical issue in a passage. Next, you've underscored the qualitative issue in the passage. Then, you've accepted that you may need additional help to offer a practical solution. Now, it is time to narrow down what you think can be done to address the parts of the manuscript that require additional review.

To offer a fix for the issue or guidance for next steps, you need to narrow down what you think the impact will be if the author doesn't review or address the issue you've noticed, underscored, and accepted. To have the best results, and to give the author an opinion on why you think the issue needs to be addressed, you have to connect the dots by offering an explanation of what could happen without further review. You need to show the author a possible consequence of what happens if the passage is left as is.

When done appropriately, narrowing down the possible consequences will allow the author to see what their options are. In the "Notice" exercise, you identified content in a passage that did not match your expectations. Now, in this "Narrow" exercise, you are giving the author your perspective on what could happen without considering your guidance. Remember, your guidance is for the author's consideration; it is not a mandate. This is only a consideration, because what you identified as a possible issue may not be an actual issue or problem. Since you are not sure if there is more to this potential issue than you understand, you can only offer your idea of what you think should be done based on the expertise and knowledge that you have. The author may have additional information that could override your concerns, and that is okay. The point is to remind the author that you are on their side to get the manuscript done right, and that they still have an active role in this process. The author must weigh your queries against their own expertise and make a determination. This is why your guidance is important. Identifying a possible consequence is a tangible piece of guidance that will help the author make the final decision. Giving the author something that they can work with and take action on will serve them better in the long run, rather than merely pointing out a problem and suggesting they fix it.

The guidance in this part of the process is crucial, because the last thing you want to do is leave the writer flailing. Without any direction at all, you run the risk of the writer not knowing what to do. Remember, the writer is counting on your expertise to get through this editing and revision process. You don't want them feeling like there wasn't much to doing this work. You did a lot of invisible work. While you may not know the exact thing to do, the guidance you can offer can still serve the writer if approached properly.

Your Action: Narrow down the parts that action could be taken on.

Your Approach: Think Tangible.

	What to Do	How to Phrase It
N – Narrow	**Think *Tangible*:** Identify the impact that you suspect will happen if the issue is not addressed.	I ask because I think that [passage] will [insert consequence] unless [specific action is taken].
	Ask Yourself: Is there a tangible consequence to leaving something unaddressed? If so, what is it?	

C – Consult

Now, it is important here to remember that for some aspects of the manuscript, you are not the expert. While part of the guidance you offered in the "Narrow" exercise lays out your opinion on the potential consequences of not considering the query, you still don't have all the answers. Depending on the type of manuscript you are working on, your writer may be the expert on its content or, at least, likely more knowledgeable than you are, assuming due diligence is done.

It is important to know that the writer's expertise may not be formal in the way of a degree or an award that they've won; but that doesn't mean it isn't there! It's also important not to assume that they don't have awards and a big name or other visible credentials. Just because they are new to you doesn't mean that they are new, especially to their target audience. As the saying goes, sometimes you don't know what you don't know. You are likely equipped to handle many of the different types of manuscripts out there on different subjects. But it is just as important to acknowledge when you aren't.

This is where consulting comes in.

There are two ways you can consult other sources. You can either do a cursory (quick) search on the internet and look for information that may help give you — the editor — insight on the issue that you're thinking about (this is arguably the harder option). Or, you can consult the writer, since they are much more likely to have the background knowledge that you do not.

A quick internet search may be helpful to you, but it may not be so for the author. The author, in most cases, will already know what the top results in the search engine are, and they may not be the most relevant or useful to the author's point. However, the top results in the search engine may reveal information that will give you some idea of the scope of what the author is writing about. This additional information may help you ask follow-up questions or confirm that you definitely need the author's help to resolve the query. This is why asking the author what they think is a good idea. When phrased delicately, it reinforces that you value their knowledge in this process and that what they know matters.

Consulting via a quick internet search should either: help you clarify just enough to know if you can assist with resolving the query or confirm that you can't make the editorial call. An internet search is not an opportunity to "prove a point" to the writer. Do not insult the author by suggesting that whatever and whoever is on the internet knows more than they do. Consulting via asking the author is a mindful solution. This is a strategy to help you gain just enough clarity to make an informed decision about the guidance that you are about to give.

Based on what you find (or don't find), you should revise or tweak your query, and provide a source or reference as necessary (so that the writer knows where your thoughts are coming from). Since you may not know if the information is correct, it gives the writer a benchmark to understand your thinking. Perhaps something you find (or don't) can help the writer assess whether or not your suggestion makes sense for them. The author retains the ability to make the final call. But without context, the author may not know if you recognize that an internet search is rarely enough to make a decision on the direction of the query. Even if you are trying to fact-check something that you suspect is wrong, you still need to ask the author if what you've found makes sense for the context. It is not uncommon for out-of-date or incorrect information to persistently remain highly visible on the internet.

Furthermore, it is important to remember that many writers, especially ones from marginalized backgrounds, are often told through a variety of ways that they are not the experts on their own content and that they must always concede to someone else's thoughts, opinions, and suggestions. They are often told that they are not authorities on what they write and are regularly dismissed. It is neither prudent nor your job to disregard the author's authority. Your job is to provide guidance that still honors the work they have put in and recognizes their knowledge and experiences.

Your Action: Consult other resources to better understand what you may be working with.

Your Approach: Think Mindful.

	What to Do	**How to Phrase It**
C – Consult	**Think *Mindful*:** Do a quick internet search on the issue from the manuscript that you think needs to be addressed. **Ask Yourself:** Would any outside information that you find possibly help you with making a decision on what to ask the author?	Do you think that [source] is applicable in this situation? How do you feel about the way [example] addressed this scenario?

E – Empower

This. It all leads up to this. This is where you break the cycle. This is where you tell the writer, in the query, that they make the ultimate decision as to what happens next.

This has been a fruitful process of channeling respect, guidance, and action into querying that will really change your relationship with writers from many backgrounds as well as your relationship with editing. You are sharing your power with someone who needs it to do their best work. The final step in this query is reminding the author that this is an excellent opportunity to step up and reclaim power that should have never been taken away through many instances of over-editing. As an editor, you are their partner in bringing their manuscript into the best shape it can be.

On the surface, this empowerment sounds like only encouragement — like a cheerleader for the writer. While I bet you do want the writer to "win," your job description probably doesn't say "encourage writers to do their best." Cheering someone on isn't enough to make sure that they put forth their best work. They need actionable steps and to be reminded that this journey is theirs and that you are an actor in their success.

This is empowerment. Empowerment is an authoritative solution. You are removing some barriers for the author so that they may finish the manuscript on their terms. You are not the gatekeeper of their knowledge, their manuscript, or this process. You are letting the author know that it is important for them to use your guidance — if you were able to offer any — and reminding them of their power to make the final decision.

This may seem obvious to most editors, but it may not be so for the author. Most writers never get used to being told that they are wrong or that something they've written doesn't make sense. And it isn't always true! But, for folks from marginalized backgrounds, there are extra layers of disempowerment that are built up long before they start working with you. These layers may not be visible to you, but they exist and may be masked by the writing in the manuscript that you receive.

Many editors don't always recognize the amount of power that they have over a writer's work. Especially as a freelance editor, you may be used to having a largely invisible role in the process. In some cases, your name may never be revealed to a larger audience, so people may not be aware that you worked on a manuscript. But make no mistake, your work shaped the final product. You can either be the editor who advocated for the writer to honor their expertise and polish it for its final audience, or you can be the editor who unknowingly sucked the life out of the manuscript by obtrusively imposing standards that didn't make sense for the work at hand. It sounds dramatic, but it happens all the time. Sometimes the author may share what happened and their resulting discontent down the line — but many do not. For longer pieces, like books, folks may be secretly upset about how their work turned out and that they published a book that they were not truly proud of. For shorter pieces, like an article for a digital or print outlet, the author may choose to pull the piece and it never gets published at all.

You may not realize your hand in these outcomes because, oftentimes, they happen long after the invoice has been paid and you've moved on to other projects. But the effect lasts. Print lives, and there is a nearly invisible record of the work that you've done. It's important to make it the best work possible. You may also gain a fruitful and productive new relationship for the future.

Let the author know that their voice matters and enable them to make the choices that are right for them and their work.

Your Action: Empower the author to make the final call.

Your Approach: Think Authoritative.

	What to Do	**How to Phrase It**
E – Empower	**Think *Authoritative*:** Let the author know that their knowledge is important and may be the key to resolving any potential issues quickly. **Ask Yourself:** Am I giving the author useful tools to move forward?	I know you will make the right call on addressing . . . I trust that your decision will be the correct one for . . . ***End with:*** If I can further help clarify this, please let me know.

NUANCE in Practice

When is editing just editing? When is querying just querying? Are you asking questions to really understand the manuscript, or are you in a hurry to work through it so that you can move onto something else? The motivations you have behind what you query, how often, and why are important and can really facilitate a productive conversation between you and the writer. Or, it can be a transaction and nothing more.

Querying is a simple but powerful tool that can really make a difference in the direction a manuscript takes. More importantly, it can transform a relationship with an author, especially one that does not share your background and experiences.

What does NUANCE look like in practice? Let's work with an example. Here's an excerpt from the novel *Somewhat Close to Normal*.

> *It's a time when spirits soar. Summertime becomes even more desirable than springtime. People make plans to go away, and many people actually manage to do so. But others end up hanging around the old neighborhood or barrio, depending on where in New York City you are from.*
>
> *Young men in their second- and third-hand Dodge Neons and Nissan Altimas are blasting hip hop, rap, salsa, merengue, reggaetón, or soca as they race down the streets. Young women and girls are wearing poom-poom shorts, skintight denim capris, booty-shorts, halters, and tube tops. They spend their time ignoring or intriguing the men*

in the cars who are shouting at them while driving down the street at about five miles per hour.

For this passage, the editor of this book used a simple query to ask about "poom-poom shorts." The editor wrote, *"Is this right? I couldn't find a reference for poom-poom."* That was the entire query. A little more direction may have saved it from being cut from the final version of the manuscript. Instead, "booty-shorts" was the term that remained and "poom-poom" (a suggestive term that has several interpretations) was eliminated from the published version. While this is arguably an acceptable revision, with a little more direction, the term may have appeared as it was originally written in the draft. It is likely that it was eliminated to avoid explaining a term that was not intended to be understood by every reader.

To compare, let's use NUANCE to re-write the query.

N – I noticed that "poom-poom" was used to describe the type of shorts women are wearing.

U – In particular, it is unclear to me if "poom-poom" is an informal term used in the setting.

A – I am not familiar with this term.

N – Is it a term that is regional to New York City? I ask, since I am not sure if this term reflects a dialect, or if it was a true typo.

C – Do you think it would take away from the dialogue to refer to it as short-shorts or Daisy Dukes? I did a quick internet search and did not come up with anything comparable to "poom-poom shorts" so this is my best guess. I defer to you, as I do not want to take away from the character's voice, especially if it is distinct to the character or the region.

E – Either way, I know that whatever decision you make will reflect well on the character. The intended audience will likely recognize what you mean.

This query is much clearer on what the question is and why it is being asked. This query, built with NUANCE, hints at understanding that there may be a level to the piece that was outside the editor's understanding. It offered questions to help the author think about how the piece may be read and allowed for the possibilities that the editor was not able

Respectful Querying with NUANCE

to pinpoint. A query built this way respectfully offers guidance without assuming too much.

Querying with NUANCE can help an author reach their goals without compromising their expertise or their work. The next time you encounter content that doesn't fit what you'd expect, consider building a query with NUANCE to address what you find and help the author build a solution when required.

About the Author

 **Ebonye Gussine Wilkins** is a social justice writer, editor, and media activist shaping media through the lens of inclusion. She is the founder and Chief Executive Officer of Inclusive Media Solutions LLC. Packaging solutions to be thoughtful, accurate, and restorative, Ebonye works with people to shift the focus toward what we can do *right now* to make content more inclusive. She partners with people to help align their goals with the communities they seek to represent and create solutions with. Ebonye brings together good people and good companies to create media that heals and empowers.

About the Editorial Freelancers Association (EFA)

Celebrating 50 Years!
Dedicated to the Education and Growth
of Editorial Freelancers

The EFA is a national not-for-profit—501(c)6—organization, headquartered in New York City, run by member volunteers, all of whom are also freelancers. The EFA's members, experienced in a wide range of professional skills, live and work all across the United States and in other countries.

A pioneer in organizing freelancers into a network for mutual support and advancement, the EFA is now recognized throughout the publishing industry as the source for professional editorial assistance.

We welcome people of every race, color, culture, religion or no religion, gender identity, gender expression, age, national or ethnic origin, ancestry, citizenship, education, ability, health, neurotype, marital/parental status, socio-economic background, sexual orientation, and/or military status. We are nothing without our members, and encourage everyone to volunteer and to participate in our community.

The EFA sells a variety of specialized booklets, not unlike this one, on topics of interest to editorial freelancers at the-efa.org.

The EFA hosts online, asynchronous courses, real-time webinars, and on-demand recorded webinars designed especially for freelance editors, writers, and other editorial specialists around the world. You can learn more about our Education Program at the-efa.org.

To learn about these and other EFA offerings, visit the-efa.org and join us on social media:

Twitter: @EFAFreelancers
Instagram: @efa_editors
Facebook: editorialfreelancersassociation
LinkedIn: editorial-freelancers

www.ingramcontent.com/pod-product-compliance
Lightning Source LLC
Chambersburg PA
CBHW071549080526
44588CB00011B/1848